MELODY • LYRICS • CHORDS

SEA SHANTIES

Hal Leonard
7777 West Bluemound Road
Milwaukee, WI 53213
Email: info@halleonard.com

ISBN 978-1-70513-511-2

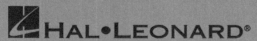

Visit Hal Leonard Online at
www.halleonard.com

Contact us:
Hal Leonard
7777 West Bluemound Road
Milwaukee, WI 53213
Email: info@halleonard.com

In Europe, contact:
Hal Leonard Europe Limited
42 Wigmore Street
Marylebone, London, W1U 2RN
Email: info@halleonardeurope.com

In Australia, contact:
Hal Leonard Australia Pty. Ltd.
4 Lentara Court
Cheltenham, Victoria, 3192 Australia
Email: info@halleonard.com.au

4 Blood Red Roses

5 Blow the Man Down

6 The Bonnie Ship The Diamond

8 Bound for South Australia

10 The Coasts of High Barbary

9 Don't Forget Your Old Shipmate

12 The Drunken Sailor

14 Eliza Lee

16 Fiddler's Green

15 Haul Away, Joe

18 John Kanaka

19 Leave Her, Johnny

20 Lowlands Away

21 The Mermaid

23 Nassau Bound

22 Paddy Doyle's Boots

26 Randy Dandy-O

27 Roll the Old Chariot Along

28 Roll the Woodpile Down

30 Rolling Down to Old Maui

29 Sally Brown

32 Santiana

33 Shenandoah

38 Song of the Vikings

34 Spanish Ladies

36 Wellerman

BLOOD RED ROSES

Sea Chantey

BLOW THE MAN DOWN

Traditional Sea Chantey

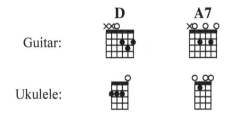

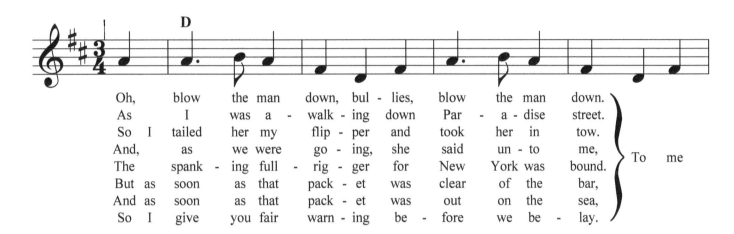

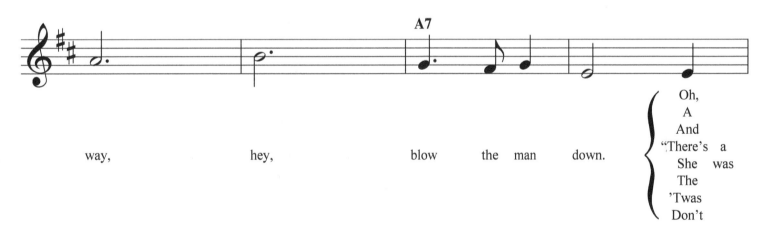

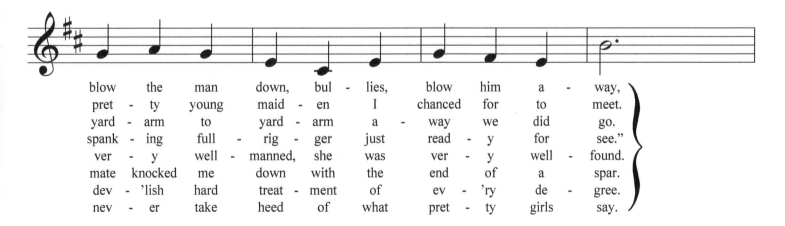

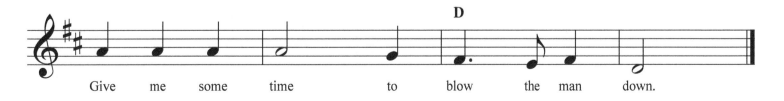

THE BONNIE SHIP THE DIAMOND

Traditional

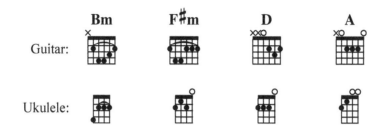

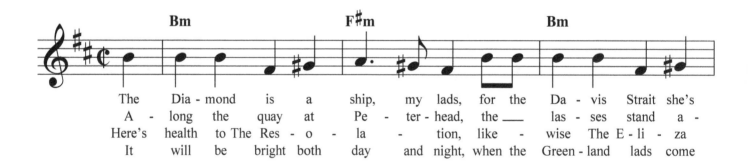

The Dia - mond is a ship, my lads, for the Da - vis Strait she's
A - long the quay at Pe - ter - head, the ___ las - ses stand a -
Here's health to The Res - o - la - tion, like - wise The E - li - za
It will be bright both day and night, when the Green - land lads come

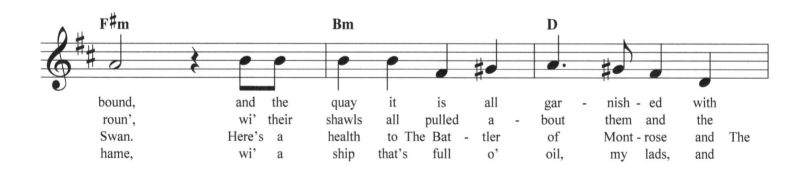

bound, and the quay it is all gar - nish - ed with
roun', wi' their shawls all pulled a - bout them and the
Swan. Here's a health to The Bat - tler of Mont - rose and The
hame, wi' a ship that's full o' oil, my lads, and

bon - nie las - ses round. Cap - tain Thom - son gives the
salt tears run - nin' down. Don't you weep my bon - nie
Dia - mond, ship ___ of fame. We ___ wear the trou - sers
mon - ey to ___ our name. We'll ___ make the cra - dles

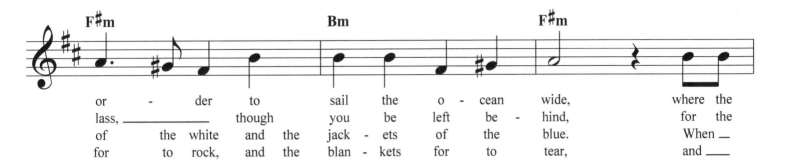

or - der to sail the o - cean wide, where the
lass, _____ though you be left be - hind, for the
of the white and the jack - ets of the blue. When _
for to rock, and the blan - kets for to tear, and _

sun it nev - er sets, my lad, no dark - nesss dims _ the
rose will grow on Green - land's ice be - fore we change _ our
we re - turn to Pe - ter - head we'll ha'e sweet - hearts _ e -
ev - ry lass in Pe - ter - head sing, "Hush - a - bye, _ my

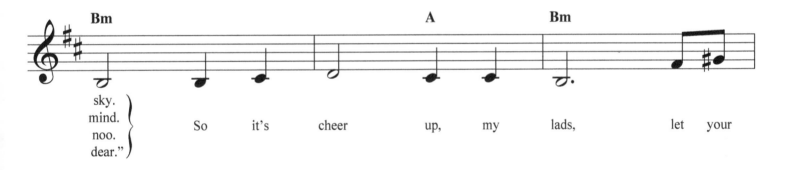

sky.
mind.
noo.
dear." }
So it's cheer up, my lads, let your

hearts nev - er fail, while the bon - nie ship The

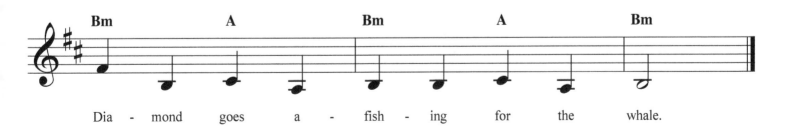

Dia - mond goes a - fish - ing for the whale.

BOUND FOR SOUTH AUSTRALIA

Australian Sea Chantey

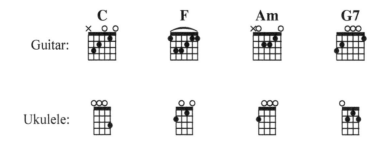

Oh, South Aus - tra - lia's my na - tive home, heave a -

way, heave a - way. Oh South Aus - tra - lia's

my na - tive home, we're bound for South Aus - tra - lia.

Heave a - way, heave a - way. Oh, heave a - way you

ru - ler King, we're bound for South Aus - tra - lia.

DON'T FORGET YOUR OLD SHIPMATE

Traditional

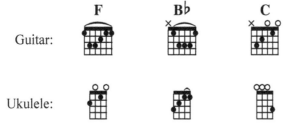

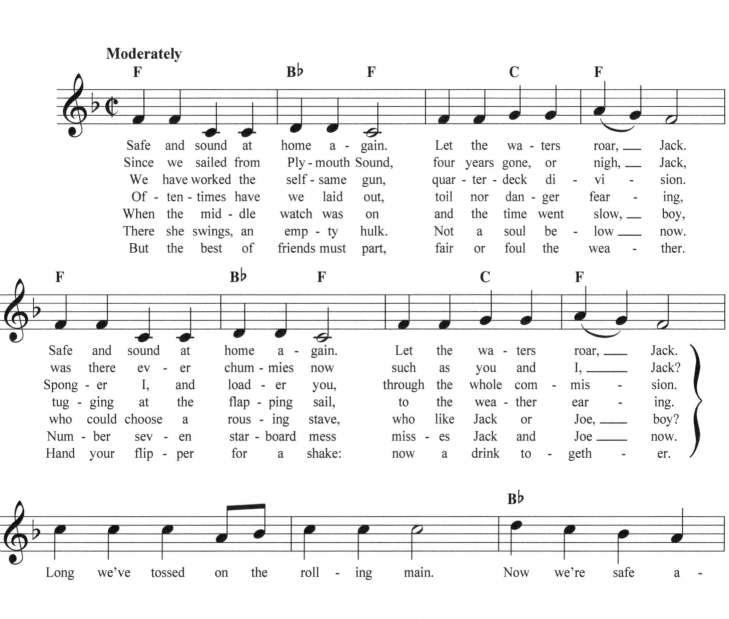

Moderately

Safe and sound at home a - gain. Let the wa - ters roar, ___ Jack.
Since we sailed from Ply - mouth Sound, four years gone, or nigh, ___ Jack,
We have worked the self - same gun, quar - ter - deck di - vi - sion.
Of - ten - times have we laid out, toil nor dan - ger fear - ing,
When the mid - dle watch was on and the time went slow, ___ boy,
There she swings, an emp - ty hulk. Not a soul be - low ___ now.
But the best of friends must part, fair or foul the wea - ther.

Safe and sound at home a - gain. Let the wa - ters roar, ___ Jack.
was there ev - er chum - mies now such as you and I, ___ Jack?
Spong - er I, and load - er you, through the whole com - mis - sion.
tug - ging at the flap - ping sail, to the wea - ther ear - ing.
who could choose a rous - ing stave, who like Jack or Joe, ___ boy?
Num - ber sev - en star - board mess miss - es Jack and Joe ___ now.
Hand your flip - per for a shake: now a drink to - geth - er.

Long we've tossed on the roll - ing main. Now we're safe a -

shore, ___ Jack. Don't for - get your old ship - mate.

Fal - dee ral - dee ral - dee ral - dee rye - eye - doe!

THE COASTS OF HIGH BARBARY

Sixteenth Century English Sea Chanty

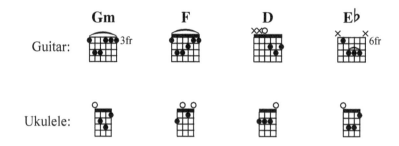

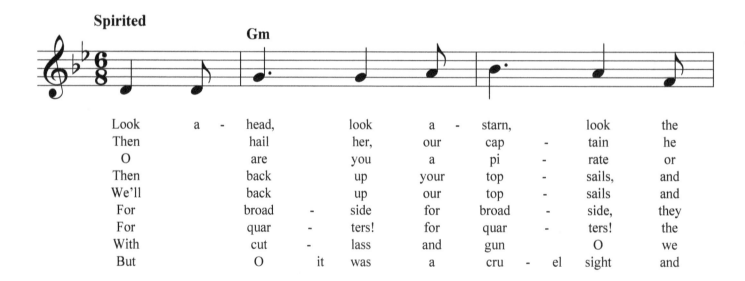

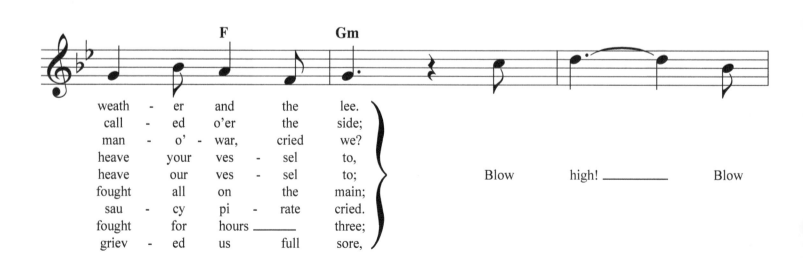

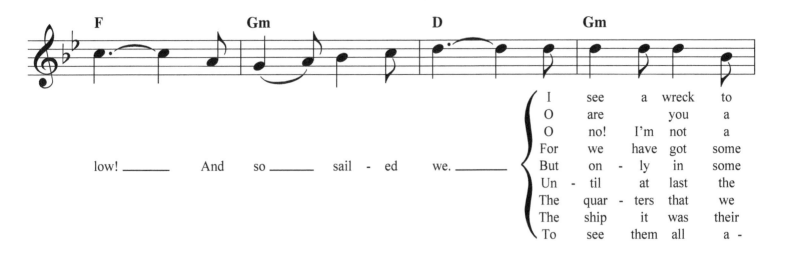

I see a wreck to
O are you a
O no! I'm not a
For we have got some
But on - ly in some
Un - til at last the
The quar - ters that we
The ship it was their
To see them all a -

low! _____ And so _____ sail - ed we. _____

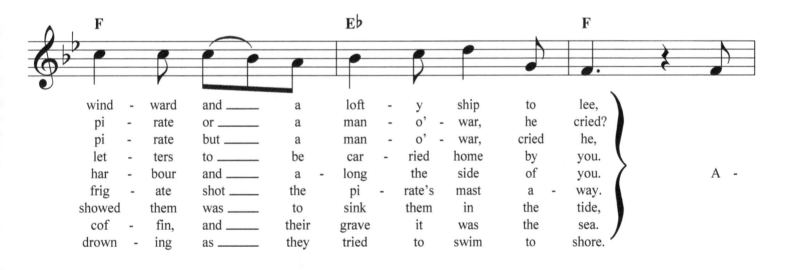

wind - ward and _____ a loft - y ship to lee,
pi - rate or _____ a man - o' - war, he cried?
pi - rate but _____ a man - o' - war, cried he,
let - ters to _____ be car - ried home by you.
har - bour and _____ a - long the side of you.
frig - ate shot _____ the pi - rate's mast a - way.
showed them was _____ to sink them in the tide,
cof - fin, and _____ their grave it was the sea.
drown - ing as _____ they tried to swim to shore.

A -

sail - ing down all on the coasts of High Bar - ba - ry.

THE DRUNKEN SAILOR

American Sea Chantey

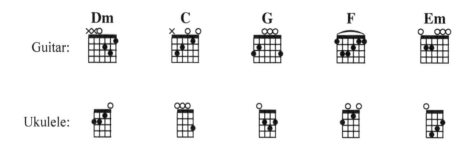

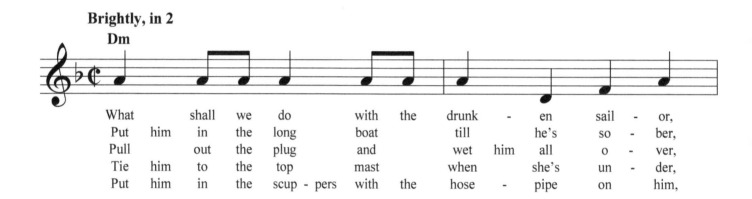

Brightly, in 2

Dm

What shall we do with the drunk - en sail - or,
Put him in the long boat till he's so - ber,
Pull out the plug and wet him all o - ver,
Tie him to the top mast when she's un - der,
Put him in the scup - pers with the hose - pipe on him,

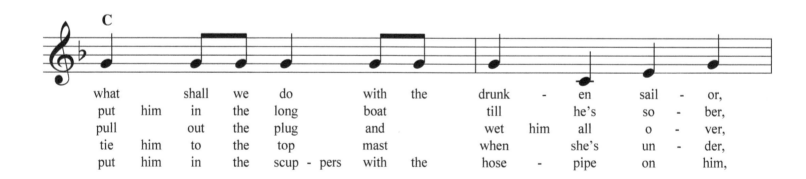

C

what shall we do with the drunk - en sail - or,
put him in the long boat till he's so - ber,
pull out the plug and wet him all o - ver,
tie him to the top mast when she's un - der,
put him in the scup - pers with the hose - pipe on him,

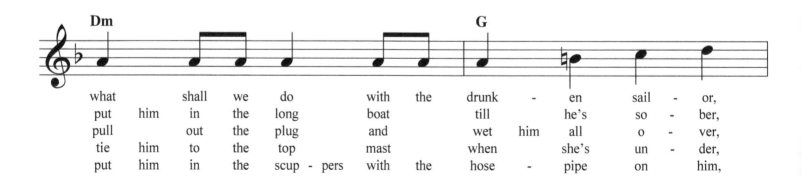

Dm   **G**

what shall we do with the drunk - en sail - or,
put him in the long boat till he's so - ber,
pull out the plug and wet him all o - ver,
tie him to the top mast when she's un - der,
put him in the scup - pers with the hose - pipe on him,

13

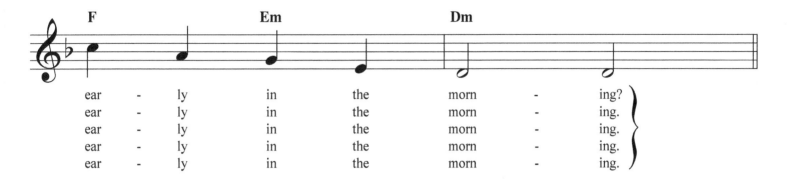

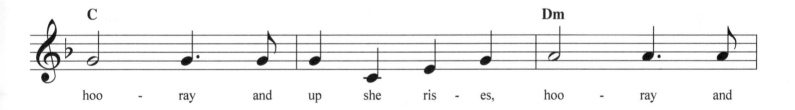

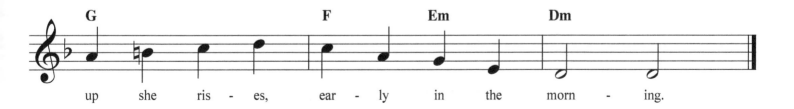

ELIZA LEE

Traditional

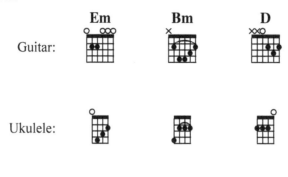

Moderately fast

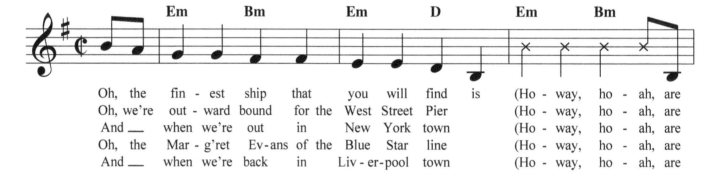

Oh, the fin - est ship that you will find is (Ho - way, ho - ah, are
Oh, we're out - ward bound for the West Street Pier (Ho - way, ho - ah, are
And __ when we're out in New York town (Ho - way, ho - ah, are
Oh, the Mar - g'ret Ev-ans of the Blue Star line (Ho - way, ho - ah, are
And __ when we're back in Liv-er-pool town (Ho - way, ho - ah, are

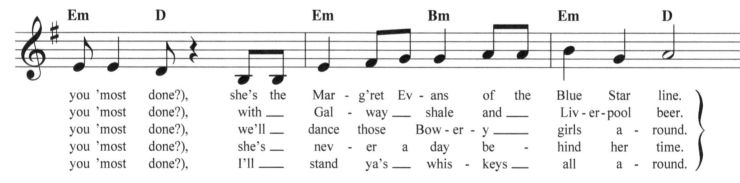

you 'most done?), she's the Mar - g'ret Ev - ans of the Blue Star line.
you 'most done?), with __ Gal - way __ shale and __ Liv-er-pool beer.
you 'most done?), we'll __ dance those Bow-er - y _____ girls a - round.
you 'most done?), she's __ nev - er a day be - hind her time.
you 'most done?), I'll __ stand ya's __ whis - keys __ all a - round.

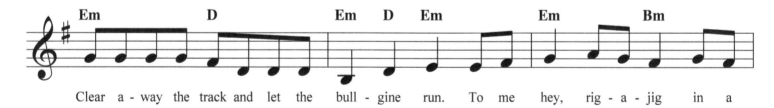

Clear a - way the track and let the bull - gine run. To me hey, rig - a - jig in a

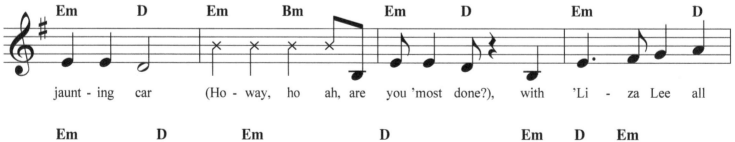

jaunt - ing car (Ho - way, ho - ah, are you 'most done?), with 'Li - za Lee all

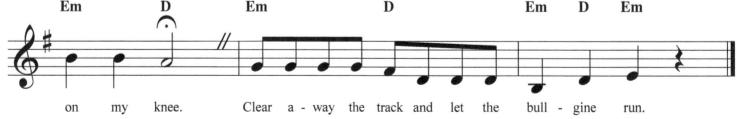

on my knee. Clear a - way the track and let the bull - gine run.

HAUL AWAY, JOE

Traditional

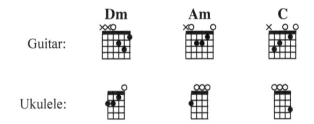

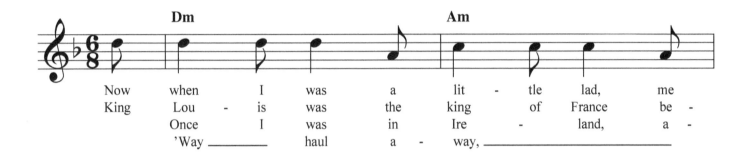

Now when I was a lit - tle lad, me
King Lou - is was the king of France be -
Once I was in Ire - land, a -
'Way _____ haul a - way, _____

moth - er al - ways told _____ me that if I don't kiss the
fore the Re - vo - lu - tion. And then _____ he got his
dig - ging turf and ta - ties, but now _____ I'm on a
rock and roll me o - ver. 'Way _____ haul a -

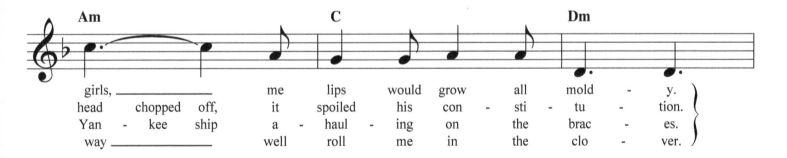

girls, _____ me lips would grow all mold - y.
head chopped off, it spoiled his con - sti - tu - tion.
Yan - kee ship a - haul - ing on the brac - es.
way _____ well roll me in the clo - ver.

'Way haul a - way, _____ we'll haul for fin - er weath - er. _____

'Way, haul a - way, _____ we'll haul a - way, Joe. _____

FIDDLER'S GREEN

Traditional Irish Folk Song

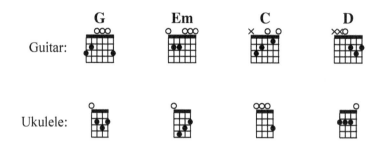

Guitar:

Ukulele:

Moderately

G   Em

As I walked by the dock - side one eve - nin' so rare _____
Now, Fid - ler's _ Green is a place I've heard tell _____
And when you're in dock and the long trip is through, _____
Now, don't want a harp, nor a ha - lo, not me. _____

G   C   G

_____ to view the still wa - ters and take the salt
_____ where fish - er - men go if they don't go to
_____ there's pubs and there's clubs and there's las - sies there,
_____ Just give me a breeze and a good roll - in'

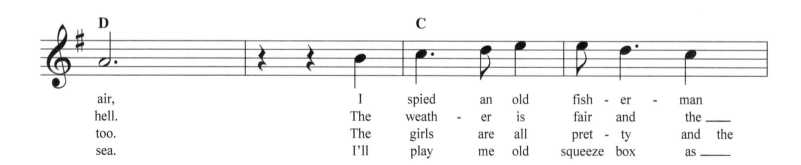

D   C

air, I spied an old fish - er - man
hell. The weath - er is fair and the _____
too. The girls are all pret - ty and the
sea. I'll play me old squeeze box as _____

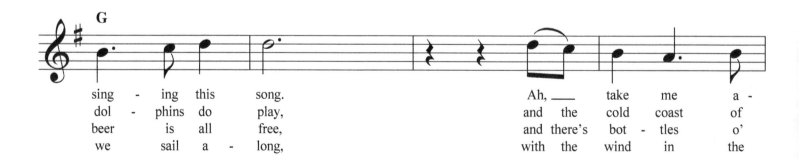

G

sing - ing this song. Ah, _____ take me a -
dol - phins do play, and the cold coast of
beer is all free, and there's bot - tles o'
we sail a - long, with the wind in the

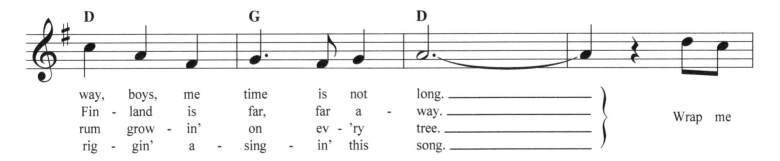

way, boys, me time is not long. _____ Wrap me
Fin - land is far, far a - way. _____
rum grow - in' on ev - 'ry tree. _____
rig - gin' a - sing - in' this song. _____

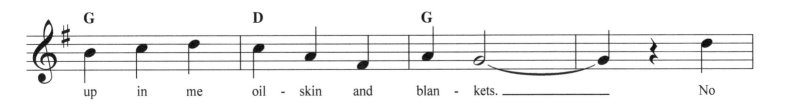

up in me oil - skin and blan - kets. _____ No

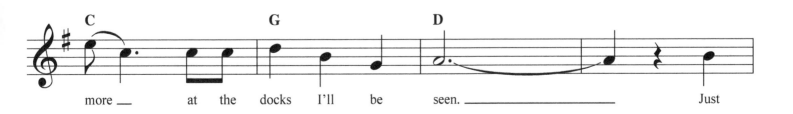

more __ at the docks I'll be seen. _____ Just

tell me old ship - mates I'm tak - ing a trip. Mates,

I'll see ya some - day in Fid - dler's _ Green. _____

JOHN KANAKA

American Sea Chantey

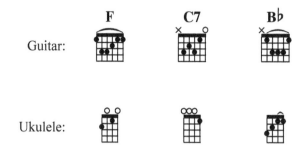

Moderately fast

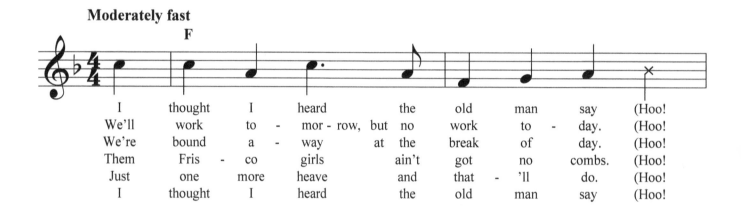

I thought I heard the old man say (Hoo!
We'll work to - mor - row, but no work to - day. (Hoo!
We're bound a - way at the break of day. (Hoo!
Them Fris - co girls ain't got no combs. (Hoo!
Just one more heave and that - 'll do. (Hoo!
I thought I heard the old man say (Hoo!

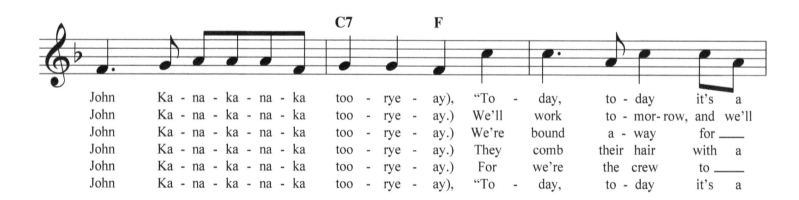

John Ka - na - ka - na - ka too - rye - ay), "To - day, to - day it's a
John Ka - na - ka - na - ka too - rye - ay.) We'll work to - mor - row, and we'll
John Ka - na - ka - na - ka too - rye - ay.) We're bound a - way for ____
John Ka - na - ka - na - ka too - rye - ay.) They comb their hair with a
John Ka - na - ka - na - ka too - rye - ay.) For we're the crew to ____
John Ka - na - ka - na - ka too - rye - ay), "To - day, to - day it's a

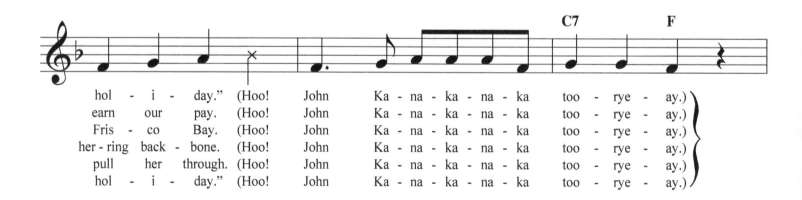

hol - i - day." (Hoo! John Ka - na - ka - na - ka too - rye - ay.)
earn our pay. (Hoo! John Ka - na - ka - na - ka too - rye - ay.)
Fris - co Bay. (Hoo! John Ka - na - ka - na - ka too - rye - ay.)
her - ring back - bone. (Hoo! John Ka - na - ka - na - ka too - rye - ay.)
pull her through. (Hoo! John Ka - na - ka - na - ka too - rye - ay.)
hol - i - day." (Hoo! John Ka - na - ka - na - ka too - rye - ay.)

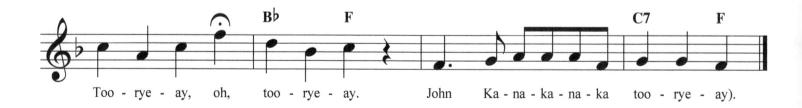

Too - rye - ay, oh, too - rye - ay. John Ka - na - ka - na - ka too - rye - ay).

LEAVE HER, JOHNNY

Traditional Sea Chantey

LOWLANDS AWAY

Traditional Scottish

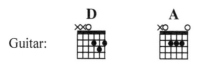

Guitar:

Ukulele:

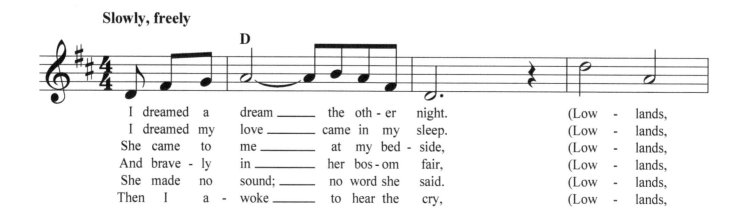

Slowly, freely

I dreamed a dream ___ the oth - er night. (Low - lands,
I dreamed my love ___ came in my sleep. (Low - lands,
She came to me ___ at my bed - side, (Low - lands,
And brave - ly in ___ her bos - om fair, (Low - lands,
She made no sound; ___ no word she said. (Low - lands,
Then I a - woke ___ to hear the cry, (Low - lands,

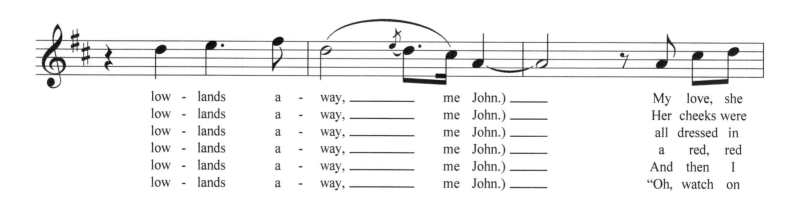

low - lands a - way, ___ me John.) ___ My love, she
low - lands a - way, ___ me John.) ___ Her cheeks were
low - lands a - way, ___ me John.) ___ all dressed in
low - lands a - way, ___ me John.) ___ a red, red
low - lands a - way, ___ me John.) ___ And then I
low - lands a - way, ___ me John.) ___ "Oh, watch on

came ___ all dressed in white. (Low - lands a - way.)
wet, ___ her eyes did weep. (Low - lands a - way.)
white, ___ like some fair bride. (Low - lands a - way.)
rose ___ my love did wear. (Low - lands a - way.)
knew ___ my love was dead. (Low - lands a - way.)
deck, ___ all hearts a - hoy." (Low - lands a - way.)

THE MERMAID

Traditional Sea Chanty

PADDY DOYLE'S BOOTS

Traditional

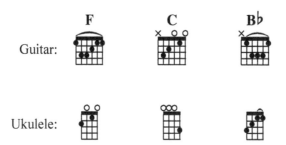

Guitar:

Ukulele:

Slowly, freely

1. To me, way - ay - ay-ay - ay, yah! We'll pay Pad-dy Doyle for his

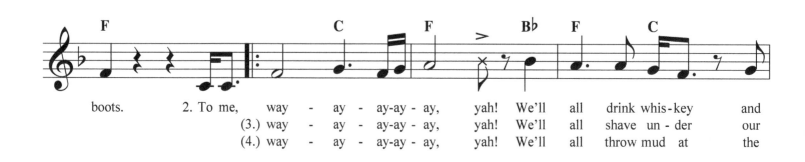

boots.   2. To me, way - ay - ay-ay - ay, yah! We'll all drink whis-key and
(3.) way - ay - ay-ay - ay, yah! We'll all shave un - der our
(4.) way - ay - ay-ay - ay, yah! We'll all throw mud at the

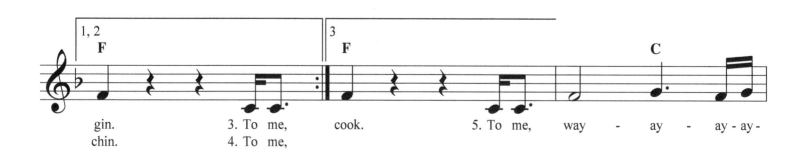

gin.   3. To me, cook.   5. To me, way - ay - ay-ay-
chin.   4. To me,

ay, yah! We'll pay Pad - dy Doyle for his boots.

NASSAU BOUND

Bahaman Sea Chanty

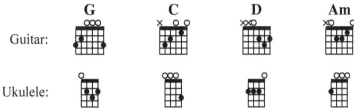

RANDY DANDY-O

Traditional

Guitar:

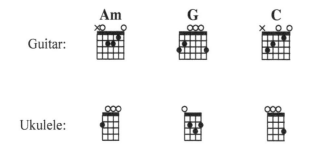

Ukulele:

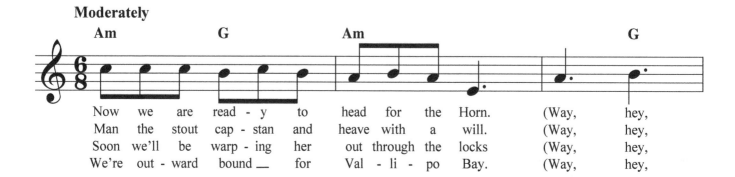

Moderately

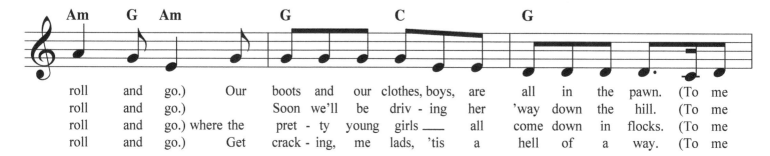

Now we are read - y to head for the Horn. (Way, hey,
Man the stout cap - stan and heave with a will. (Way, hey,
Soon we'll be warp - ing her out through the locks (Way, hey,
We're out - ward bound __ for Val - li - po Bay. (Way, hey,

roll and go.) Our boots and our clothes, boys, are all in the pawn. (To me
roll and go.) Soon we'll be driv - ing her 'way down the hill. (To me
roll and go.) where the pret - ty young girls __ all come down in flocks. (To me
roll and go.) Get crack - ing, me lads, 'tis a hell of a way. (To me

rol - lick-ing ran - dy dan - dy - O.)
rol - lick-ing ran - dy dan - dy - O.)
rol - lick-ing ran - dy dan - dy - O.)
rol - lick-ing ran - dy dan - dy - O.)

Heave a pawl __ and heave __ a - way.

(Way hey, roll and go.) The an - chor's on board and the

ca - bles all stored. (To me rol - lick-ing ran - dy dan - dy - O.)

ROLL THE OLD CHARIOT ALONG
(Drop of Nelson's Blood)

Sea Chantey

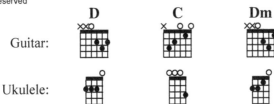

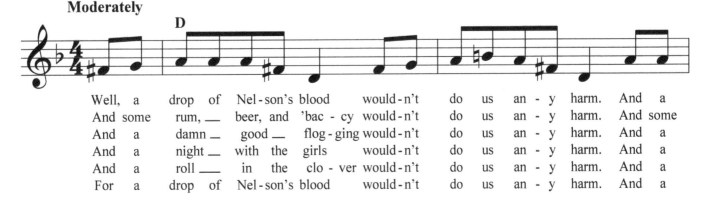

Moderately

Well, a drop of Nel-son's blood would-n't do us an-y harm. And a
And some rum, __ beer, and 'bac-cy would-n't do us an-y harm. And some
And a damn __ good __ flog-ging would-n't do us an-y harm. And a
And a night __ with the girls would-n't do us an-y harm. And a
And a roll __ in the clo-ver would-n't do us an-y harm. And a
For a drop of Nel-son's blood would-n't do us an-y harm. And a

drop of Nel-son's blood would-n't do us an-y harm. And a drop of Nel-son's blood would-n't
rum, __ beer, and 'bac-cy would-n't do us an-y harm. And some rum, __ beer, and 'bac-cy would-n't
damn _ good _ flog-ging would-n't do us an-y harm. And a damn _ good _ flog-ging would-n't
night _ with the girls would-n't do us an-y harm. And a night _ with the girls would-n't
roll __ in the clo-ver would-n't do us an-y harm. And a roll __ in the clo-ver would-n't
drop of Nel-son's blood would-n't do us an-y harm. And a drop of Nel-son's blood would-n't

do us an-y harm. And we'll all hang on be - hind. ⎫
do us an-y harm. And we'll all hang on be - hind. ⎪
do us an-y harm. And we'll all hang on be - hind. ⎬ Come on and
do us an-y harm. And we'll all hang on be - hind. ⎪
do us an-y harm. And we'll all hang on be - hind. ⎪
do us an-y harm. And we'll all hang on be - hind. ⎭

roll the old char - i - ot a - long. We'll roll the old char - i - ot a - long. We'll

roll the old char - i - ot a - long. And we'll all hang on be - hind.

ROLL THE WOODPILE DOWN

Traditional

SALLY BROWN

Traditional Irish Folk Song

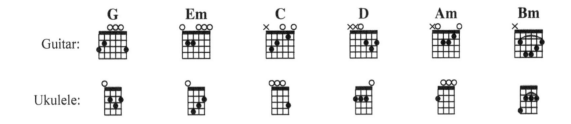

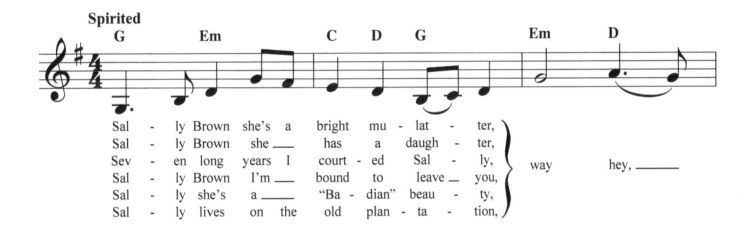

Sal - ly Brown she's a bright mu - lat - ter,
Sal - ly Brown she ___ has a daugh - ter,
Sev - en long years I court - ed Sal - ly,
Sal - ly Brown I'm ___ bound to leave ___ you,
Sal - ly she's a ___ "Ba - dian" beau - ty,
Sal - ly lives on the old plan - ta - tion,

way   hey, ___

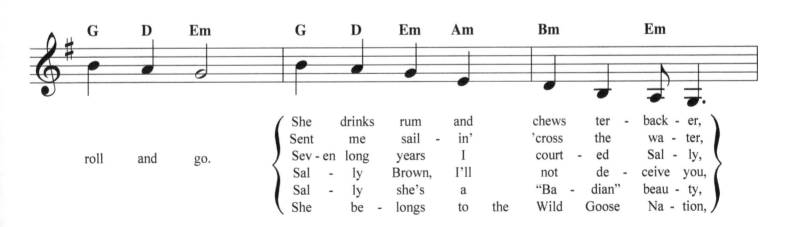

roll   and   go.

She drinks rum and chews ter - back - er,
Sent me sail - in' 'cross the wa - ter,
Sev - en long years I court - ed Sal - ly,
Sal - ly Brown, I'll not de - ceive you,
Sal - ly she's a "Ba - dian" beau - ty,
She be - longs to the Wild Goose Na - tion,

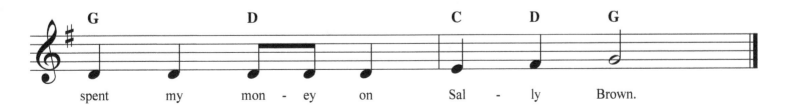

spent   my   mon - ey   on   Sal - ly   Brown.

ROLLING DOWN TO OLD MAUI

Traditional

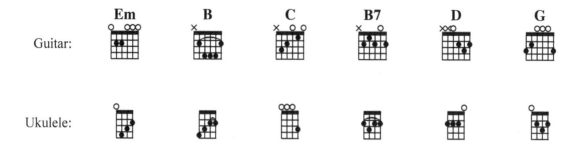

Guitar:

Ukulele:

Moderately

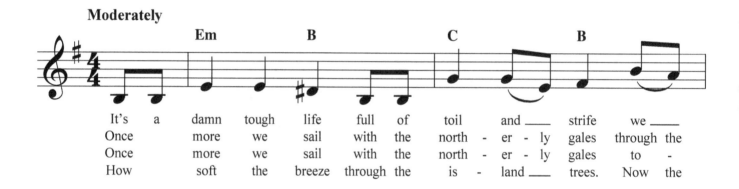

It's a damn tough life full of toil and ___ strife we ___
Once more we sail with the north - er - ly gales through the
Once more we sail with the north - er - ly gales to -
How soft the breeze through the is - land ___ trees. Now the

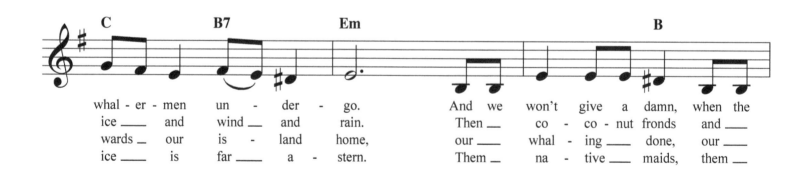

whal - er - men un - der - go. And we won't give a damn, when the
ice ___ and wind ___ and rain. Then ___ co - co - nut fronds and ___
wards ___ our is - land home, our ___ whal - ing ___ done, our ___
ice ___ is far ___ a - stern. Them ___ na - tive ___ maids, them ___

gales are ___ done, how ___ hard the winds ___ did blow. For we're
trop - i - cal shores we ___ soon shall see ___ a - gain. For six
main mast ___ sprung. Yeah, we ain't got far ___ to roam. Our ___
trop - i - cal glades is a - wait - ing our ___ re - turn. E - ven

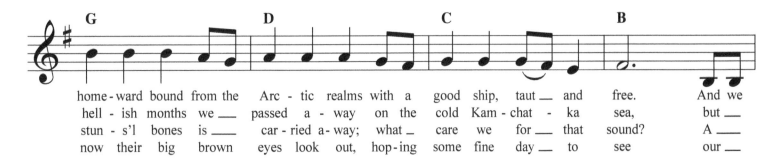

home - ward bound from the Arc - tic realms with a good ship, taut __ and free. And we
hell - ish months we __ passed a - way on the cold Kam - chat - ka sea, but __
stun - s'l bones is __ car - ried a - way; what __ care we for __ that sound? A __
now their big brown eyes look out, hop - ing some fine day __ to see our __

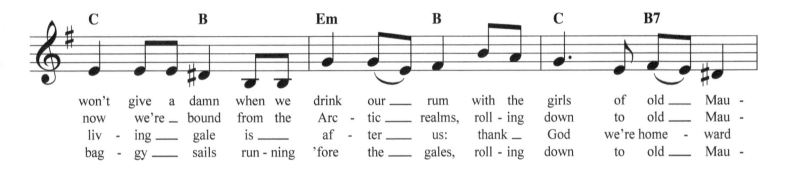

won't give a damn when we drink our __ rum with the girls of old __ Mau -
now we're __ bound from the Arc - tic __ realms, roll - ing down to old __ Mau -
liv - ing __ gale is __ af - ter __ us: thank __ God we're home - ward
bag - gy __ sails run - ning 'fore the __ gales, roll - ing down to old __ Mau -

i.
i.
bound. } Roll - ing down to old __ Mau - i, me boys, roll - ing
i.

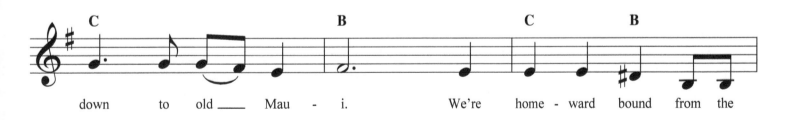

down to old __ Mau - i. We're home - ward bound from the

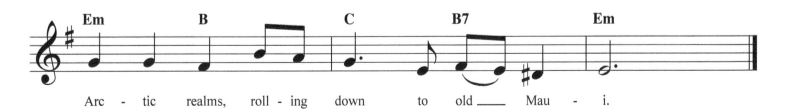

Arc - tic realms, roll - ing down to old __ Mau - i.

SANTIANA

Traditional

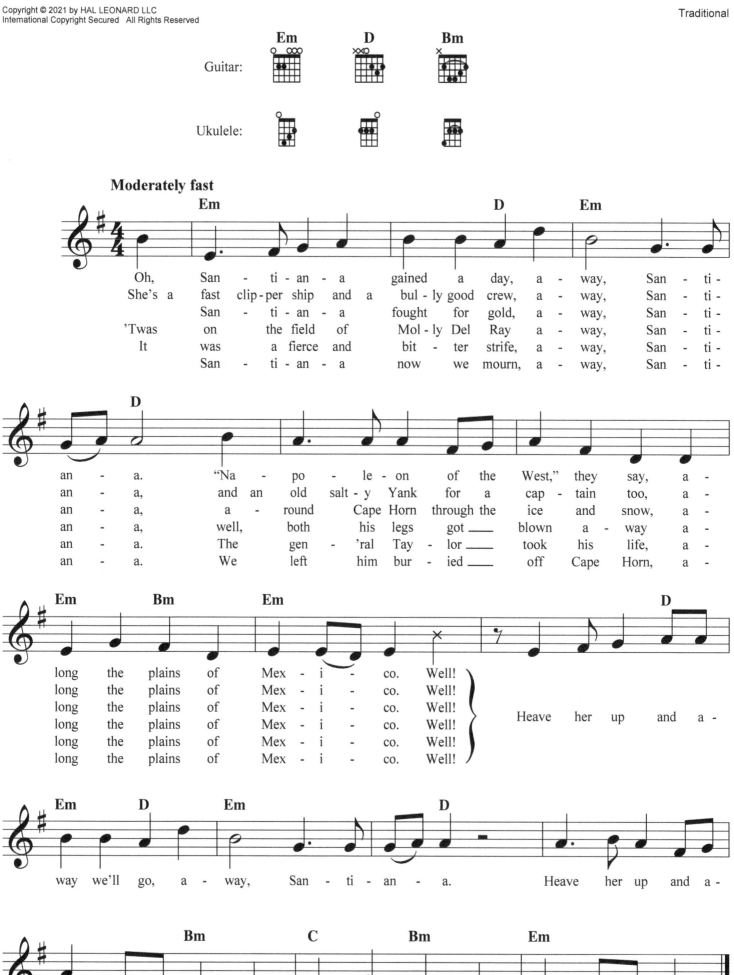

Moderately fast

Oh, San - ti - an - a gained a day, a - way, San - ti -
She's a fast clip-per ship and a bul - ly good crew, a - way, San - ti -
San - ti - an - a fought for gold, a - way, San - ti -
'Twas on the field of Mol - ly Del Ray a - way, San - ti -
It was a fierce and bit - ter strife, a - way, San - ti -
San - ti - an - a now we mourn, a - way, San - ti -

an - a. "Na - po - le - on of the West," they say, a -
an - a, and an old salt - y Yank for a cap - tain too, a -
an - a, a - round Cape Horn through the ice and snow, a -
an - a, well, both his legs got ___ blown a - way a -
an - a. The gen - 'ral Tay - lor ___ took his life, a -
an - a. We left him bur - ied ___ off Cape Horn, a -

long the plains of Mex - i - co. Well!
long the plains of Mex - i - co. Well!
long the plains of Mex - i - co. Well!
long the plains of Mex - i - co. Well!
long the plains of Mex - i - co. Well!
long the plains of Mex - i - co. Well!

Heave her up and a -

way we'll go, a - way, San - ti - an - a. Heave her up and a -

way we'll ___ go a - long the plains of Mex - i - co.

SHENANDOAH

American Folksong

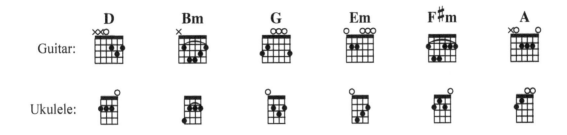

Oh, Shen - an - doah, _____ I long to hear you. _____
Oh, Shen - an - doah, _____ I love your daugh - ter. _____
Oh, Shen - an - doah, _____ I'm bound to leave you. _____
A -

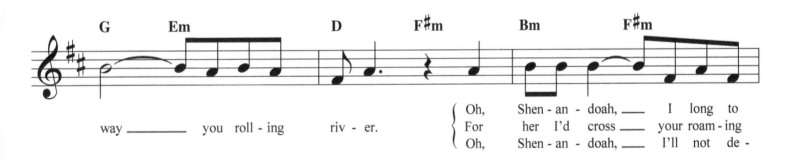

way _____ you roll - ing riv - er.
Oh, Shen - an - doah, _____ I long to
For her I'd cross _____ your roam - ing
Oh, Shen - an - doah, _____ I'll not de -

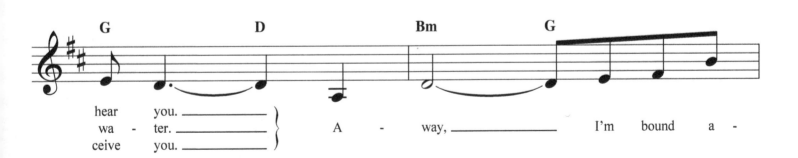

hear you. _____
wa - ter. _____
ceive you. _____
A - way, _____ I'm bound a -

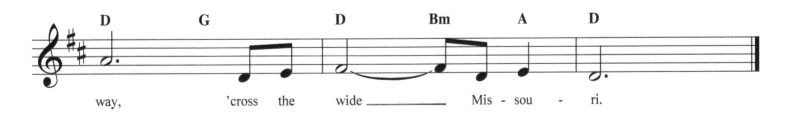

way, 'cross the wide _____ Mis - sou - ri.

SPANISH LADIES

Traditional

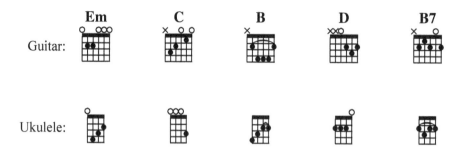

Guitar:

Ukulele:

Moderately, in 1

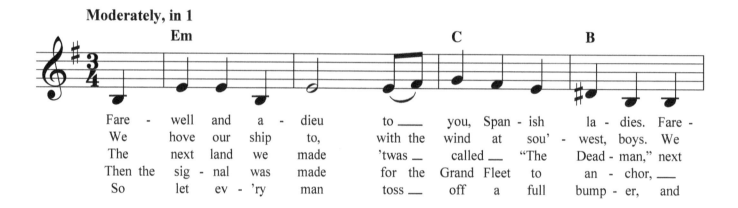

Fare - well and a - dieu to ___ you, Span - ish la - dies. Fare -
We hove our ship to, with the wind at sou' - west, boys. We
The next land we made 'twas ___ called ___ "The Dead - man," next
Then the sig - nal was made for the Grand Fleet to an - chor, ___
So let ev - 'ry man toss ___ off a full bump - er, and

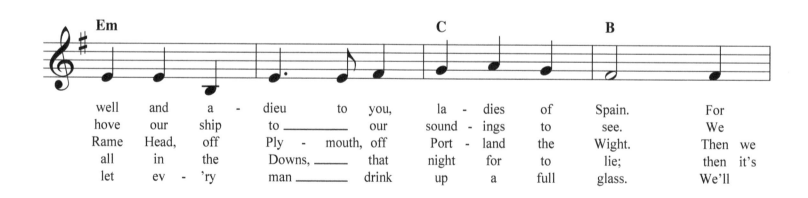

well and a - dieu to you, la - dies of Spain. For
hove our ship to _____ our sound - ings to see. We
Rame Head, off Ply - mouth, off Port - land the Wight. Then we
all in the Downs, ___ that night for to lie; then it's
let ev - 'ry man _____ drink up a full glass. We'll

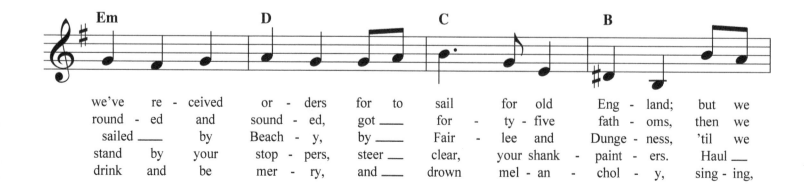

we've re - ceived or - ders for to sail for old Eng - land; but we
round - ed and sound - ed, got ___ for - ty - five fath - oms, then we
sailed ___ by Beach - y, by ___ Fair - lee and Dunge - ness, 'til we
stand by your stop - pers, steer ___ clear, your shank - paint - ers. Haul ___
drink and be mer - ry, and ___ drown mel - an - chol - y, sing - ing,

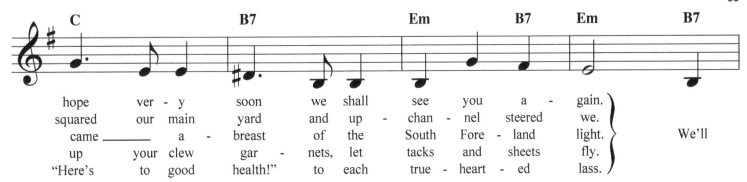

hope ver - y soon we shall see you a - gain.
squared our main yard and up - chan - nel steered we.
came _____ a - breast of the South Fore - land light.
up your clew gar - nets, let tacks and sheets fly.
"Here's to good health!" to each true - heart - ed lass.

We'll

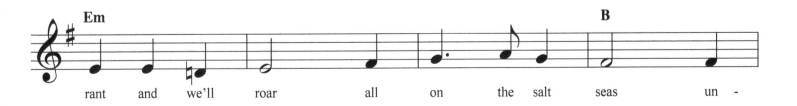

rant and we'll roar like true Brit - ish sail - ors. We'll

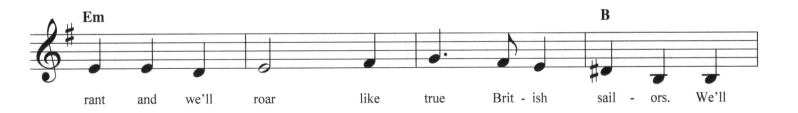

rant and we'll roar all on the salt seas un -

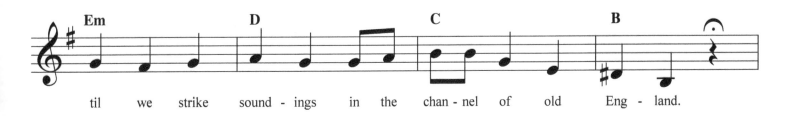

til we strike sound - ings in the chan - nel of old Eng - land.

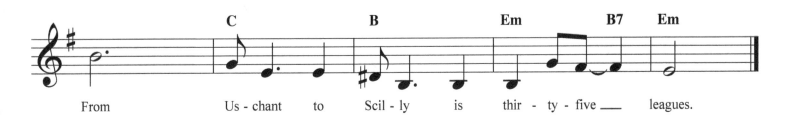

From Us - chant to Scil - ly is thir - ty-five _____ leagues.

WELLERMAN

New Zealand Folksong

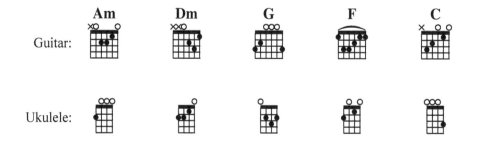

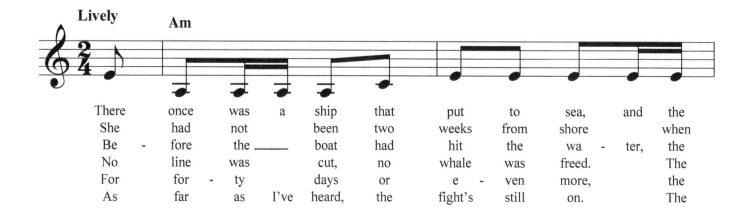

There once was a ship that put to sea, and the
She had not been two weeks from shore when
Be - fore the _____ boat had hit the wa - ter, the
No line was cut, no whale was freed. The
For for - ty days or e - ven more, the
As far as I've heard, the fight's still on. The

name of the ship was the Bil - ly of Tea. The
down on her a right whale bore. The
whale's _____ tail came _____ up _____ and caught her. All
Cap - tain's mind was not of greed, but
line went slack, then tight once more. All
line's not cut and the whale's not gone. The

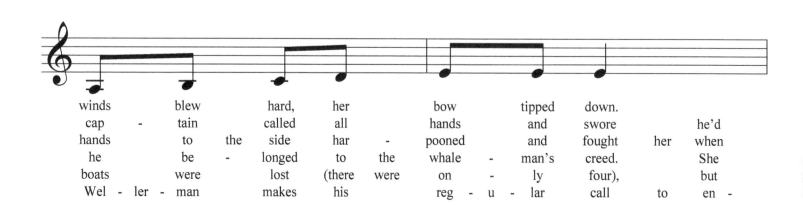

winds blew hard, her bow tipped down.
cap - tain called all hands and swore he'd
hands to the side har - pooned and fought her when
he be - longed to the whale - man's creed. She
boats were lost (there were on - ly four), but
Wel - ler - man makes his reg - u - lar call to en -

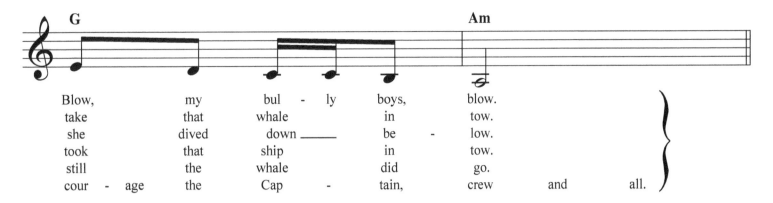

Blow, my bul - ly boys, blow.
take that whale in tow.
she dived down _____ be - low.
took that ship in tow.
still the whale did go.
cour - age the Cap - tain, crew and all.

Soon may the Wel - ler - man come to bring us sug - ar and

tea and rum. One day when the ton - guin' is done, we'll

take our leave and go.

SONG OF THE VIKINGS
(My Mother Told Me)

Traditional

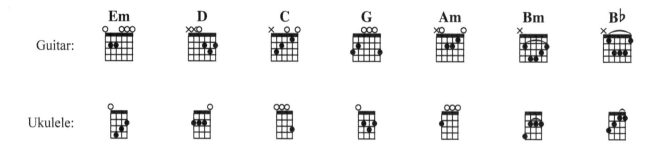

Moderately

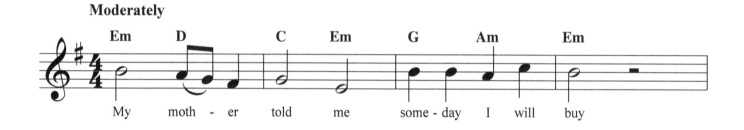

My moth - er told me some - day I will buy

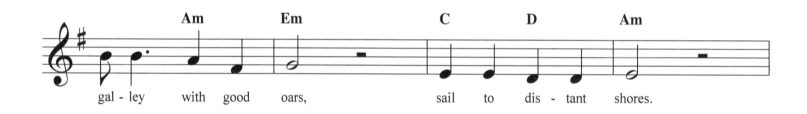

gal - ley with good oars, sail to dis - tant shores.

Stand up on ___ the prow. No - ble barque I steer.

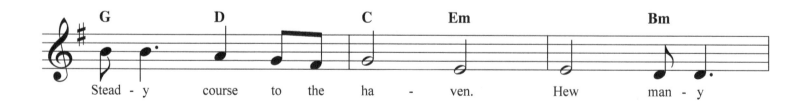

Stead - y course to the ha - ven. Hew man - y

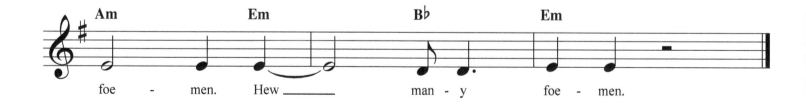

foe - men. Hew _____ man - y foe - men.

THE ULTIMATE COLLECTION OF
FAKE BOOKS

The Real Book – Sixth Edition
Hal Leonard proudly presents the first legitimate and legal editions of these books ever produced. These bestselling titles are mandatory for anyone who plays jazz! Over 400 songs, including: All By Myself • Dream a Little Dream of Me • God Bless the Child • Like Someone in Love • When I Fall in Love • and more.

00240221 Volume 1, C Instruments..$45.00
00240224 Volume 1, Bb Instruments..$45.00
00240225 Volume 1, Eb Instruments..$45.00
00240226 Volume 1, BC Instruments..$45.00

Go to **halleonard.com**
to view all *Real Books* available

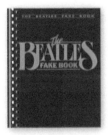

The Beatles Fake Book
200 of the Beatles' hits: All You Need Is Love • Blackbird • Can't Buy Me Love • Day Tripper • Eleanor Rigby • The Fool on the Hill • Hey Jude • In My Life • Let It Be • Michelle • Norwegian Wood (This Bird Has Flown) • Penny Lane • Revolution • She Loves You • Twist and Shout • With a Little Help from My Friends • Yesterday • and many more!
00240069 C Instruments...........$39.99

The Best Fake Book Ever
More than 1,000 songs from all styles of music: All My Loving • At the Hop • Cabaret • Dust in the Wind • Fever • Hello, Dolly • Hey Jude • King of the Road • Longer • Misty • Route 66 • Sentimental Journey • Somebody • Song Sung Blue • Spinning Wheel • Unchained Melody • We Will Rock You • What a Wonderful World • Wooly Bully • Y.M.C.A. • and more.

00290239 C Instruments.......................$49.99
00240084 Eb Instruments......................$49.95

The Celtic Fake Book
Over 400 songs from Ireland, Scotland and Wales: Auld Lang Syne • Barbara Allen • Danny Boy • Finnegan's Wake • The Galway Piper • Irish Rover • Loch Lomond • Molly Malone • My Bonnie Lies Over the Ocean • My Wild Irish Rose • That's an Irish Lullaby • and more. Includes Gaelic lyrics where applicable and a pronunciation guide.
00240153 C Instruments...........$25.00

Classic Rock Fake Book
Over 250 of the best rock songs of all time: American Woman • Beast of Burden • Carry On Wayward Son • Dream On • Free Ride • Hurts So Good • I Shot the Sheriff • Layla • My Generation • Nights in White Satin • Owner of a Lonely Heart • Rhiannon • Roxanne • Summer of '69 • We Will Rock You • You Ain't Seen Nothin' Yet • and lots more!
00240108 C Instruments.......................$35.00

Classical Fake Book
This unprecedented, amazingly comprehensive reference includes over 850 classical themes and melodies for all classical music lovers. Includes everything from Renaissance music to Vivaldi and Mozart to Mendelssohn. Lyrics in the original language are included when appropriate.
00240044.......................$39.99

The Disney Fake Book
Even more Disney favorites, including: The Bare Necessities • Can You Feel the Love Tonight • Circle of Life • How Do You Know? • Let It Go • Part of Your World • Reflection • Some Day My Prince Will Come • When I See an Elephant Fly • You'll Be in My Heart • and many more.
00175311 C Instruments...........$34.99
Disney characters & artwork TM & © 2021 Disney

The Folksong Fake Book
Over 1,000 folksongs: Bury Me Not on the Lone Prairie • Clementine • The Erie Canal • Go, Tell It on the Mountain • Home on the Range • Kumbaya • Michael Row the Boat Ashore • Shenandoah • Simple Gifts • Swing Low, Sweet Chariot • When Johnny Comes Marching Home • Yankee Doodle • and many more.
00240151 ....$34.99

The Hal Leonard Real Jazz Standards Fake Book
Over 250 standards in easy-to-read authentic hand-written jazz engravings: Ain't Misbehavin' • Blue Skies • Crazy He Calls Me • Desafinado (Off Key) • Fever • How High the Moon • It Don't Mean a Thing (If It Ain't Got That Swing) • Lazy River • Mood Indigo • Old Devil Moon • Route 66 • Satin Doll • Witchcraft • and more.
00240161 C Instruments...........................$45.00

The Hymn Fake Book
Nearly 1,000 multi-denominational hymns perfect for church musicians or hobbyists: Amazing Grace • Christ the Lord Is Risen Today • For the Beauty of the Earth • It Is Well with My Soul • A Mighty Fortress Is Our God • O for a Thousand Tongues to Sing • Praise to the Lord, the Almighty • Take My Life and Let It Be • What a Friend We Have in Jesus • and hundreds more!
00240145 C Instruments.......................$29.99

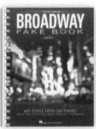

The New Broadway Fake Book
This amazing collection includes 645 songs from 285 shows: All I Ask of You • Any Dream Will Do • Close Every Door • Consider Yourself • Dancing Queen • Mack the Knife • Mamma Mia • Memory • The Phantom of the Opera • Popular • Strike up the Band • and more!
00138905 C Instruments............$45.00

The Praise & Worship Fake Book
Over 400 songs including: Amazing Grace (My Chains Are Gone) • Cornerstone • Everlasting God • Great Are You Lord • In Christ Alone • Mighty to Save • Open the Eyes of My Heart • Shine, Jesus, Shine • This Is Amazing Grace • and more.
00160838 C Instruments...........$39.99
00240324 Bb Instruments.........$34.99

Three Chord Songs Fake Book
200 classic and contemporary 3-chord tunes in melody/lyric/chord format: Ain't No Sunshine • Bang a Gong (Get It On) • Cold, Cold Heart • Don't Worry, Be Happy • Give Me One Reason • I Got You (I Feel Good) • Kiss • Me and Bobby McGee • Rock This Town • Werewolves of London • You Don't Mess Around with Jim • and more.
00240387 ....$34.99

The Ultimate Christmas Fake Book
The 6th edition of this bestseller features over 270 traditional and contemporary Christmas hits: Have Yourself a Merry Little Christmas • I'll Be Home for Christmas O Come, All Ye Faithful (Adeste Fideles) • Santa Baby • Winter Wonderland • and more.
00147215 C Instruments...........$30.00

The Ultimate Country Fake Book
This book includes over 700 of your favorite country hits: Always on My Mind • Boot Scootin' Boogie • Crazy • Down at the Twist and Shout • Forever and Ever, Amen • Friends in Low Places • The Gambler • Jambalaya • King of the Road • Sixteen Tons • There's a Tear in My Beer • Your Cheatin' Heart • and hundreds more.
00240049 C Instruments...........................$49.99

The Ultimate Fake Book
Includes over 1,200 hits: Blue Skies • Body and Soul • Endless Love • Isn't It Romantic? • Memory • Mona Lisa • Moon River • Operator • Piano Man • Roxanne • Satin Doll • Shout • Small World • Smile • Speak Softly, Love • Strawberry Fields Forever • Tears in Heaven • Unforgettable • hundreds more!
00240024 C Instruments...........$55.00
00240026 Bb Instruments.....................$49.95

The Ultimate Jazz Fake Book
This must-own collection includes 635 songs spanning all jazz styles from more than 9 decades. Songs include: Maple Leaf Rag • Basin Street Blues • A Night in Tunisia • Lullaby of Birdland • The Girl from Ipanema • Bag's Groove • I Can't Get Started • All the Things You Are • and many more!
00240079 C Instruments...............$45.00
00240080 Bb Instruments.............................$45.00
00240081 Eb Instruments.............................$45.00

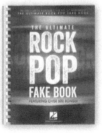

The Ultimate Rock Pop Fake Book
This amazing collection features nearly 550 rock and pop hits: American Pie • Bohemian Rhapsody • Born to Be Wild • Clocks • Dancing with Myself • Eye of the Tiger • Proud Mary • Rocket Man • Should I Stay or Should I Go • Total Eclipse of the Heart • Unchained Melody • When Doves Cry • Y.M.C.A. • You Raise Me Up • and more.
00240310 C Instruments............................$39.99

Complete songlists available online at
www.halleonard.com

HAL•LEONARD®